Tides of Expectation

Tides of Expectation

Memoir Poems

Elane Gutterman

Cover design by Shay Culligan
Cover Art by Linda Xu

ISBN: 978-1-63980-085-8

Kelsay Books
502 South 1040 East, A-119
American Fork, Utah 84003
Kelsaybooks.com

With special thanks
to poetry friends
who helped pare my poems

Acknowledgments

Grateful acknowledgement is made to the editors and publishers of the following publications in which these poems first appeared, sometimes in an earlier version:

U.S. 1 Summer Fiction Issue:
   "Carrying Water to my Indian Neighbor," "Picking Pumpkins at Grover Farm"

Paterson Literary Review (PLR):
   "Alis Grave Nil," "Hard Memories"

The New Verse News:
   "A Ghazal for Venezuela," "The Reluctant Protester, January 2018," "Toward a Gentler Good Night"

Kelsey Review:
   "Big Windows and a Patio to Catch the Light," "The Museum of Broken Relationships," "Shortness of Breath," "Watching Nomi Wrestle on YouTube," "Dancing out of Her Skin"

West Windsor Arts Center
   "Judith Scott Unbound," a shaped ekphrastic poem, was included in a juried exhibit of art inspired by other art forms in January 2015.

Contents

Postcards from Afar

Recipes for Moving

Signs of Community

Picking Pumpkins at Grover Farm

Pete Grover, West Windsor, NJ, 1921–2009

Each year, when green, withering vines
released their giant fruits,
I drove the dirt road to Mr. Grover's farm
with chatty, bouncing daughters in the back seat.
They sought lanterns for carving,
one wanted a long face,
the other searched for a rounder, less menacing form.
I took photos - rosy cheeks, flying scarves,
bright, jacketed arms lugging precious pumpkins.
We filled the trunk, brought our loot for reckoning.
Mr. Grover rose slowly from his weathered throne,
appraised pumpkins and earnest eyes to announce
his modest take. Here greed came at an affordable price.

Even after my daughters left home,
my craving for these earthy treasures continued.
I marveled at the growing games,
pumpkins in varied shapes and sizes,
the motley gourds with their furrows, warts, and twists.
In one dry season, my new car was baptized by dust.
In a wet season, my car wheels swallowed by mud,
the farmer and his tractor required to recover them.
I asked Mr. Grover if he only had to rescue
women. His wry, twinkled answer, "No."

Now, the farm across from the school grows
alfalfa and hay. Each fall I buy pumpkins
elsewhere, my thoughts with Mr. Grover.
And the town's middle school built in view of his field,
named after his son, Thomas Grover,
a purple hearted hero, dead in Vietnam,
who never had time to ripen.

Carrying Water to My Indian Neighbor

For Shefali, an Eighth Grader
"It takes a village to raise a child."

We sat on your couch
and I read your poem
all three pages.

I was struck by the lyricism
of your lines
and the vivid visual details—
> *the soft jasmine petals of a girl's beauty,*
> *jewels dripping from her fingers and throat.*

I shared these impressions
and you smiled with pride,
you probably thought
we were finished.

I asked you to read your poem aloud,
later to tell me why the beauty
and wealth of the girl
needed repeating on each page.

Quizzically, you looked at me
"My poems write themselves."
I asked you to tell me more
about the girl, her age.
You thought, said "older than me,
in her twenties."

I also asked about the "I" in the poem,
Was it a he or she?
Was there romantic interest?
What was happening
in the surroundings

as he or she became fixed
on the haunted look in the girl's eyes?

Slowly, you brought light
into the shadows,
"the young woman,
though beautiful and rich,
was unwanted by her parents."
We talked about ways
another young person
could have heard these rumors
without knowing the girl.
Now, you said, "the narrator, 'I,'
boy or girl, wanted to bring
a glimmer of light to the girl's eyes
through the hand of friendship."

In the hour I stayed,
we became two poets
cutting and smoothing
the rough spots
of a poem together.
I carried an urn, filled with the water
from years writing and studying poetry.
Now, I was bringing this water
down the street to your house.
You were refreshingly thirsty.

Toward a Gentler Good Night

*Beginning in August, terminally ill NJ patients will have the
right to end their lives,* WHYY.org, April 15, 2019

The trigger for me was the research for a poem, my artful
turn on two decades of Oregon envy, wanting their Death
with Dignity to apply in New Jersey as a lawful act.

I stumbled on the lobbying group and the way grew less abstract.
Supporters met up at the State House. Our message fine-tuned art,
we engaged lawmakers on the need for choice when near to death.

Those opposed called it suicide, minimized long-suffering death.
Finally, the bills came up for a vote, would they be enacted?
I stared at the display as votes in favor mounted like hanging art.

Work of art, my state enters the pact. Our Governor affirms
        choice in death.

Shortness of Breath

Dressed in a fedora,
tattered trousers and a jacket,
Max moved with heavy breaths
and slow steps.
He conversed with the sweep and style
of a young city man from Warsaw
before the war
though he was eighty
and about to be discharged
from a New York City hospital.
Ever the dreamer,
Max tried to grope me in the hallway
on his way to the taxi.

I was the social worker
hired to help frail patients.
I helped Max obtain a home attendant—
she said he must get rid of the boxes and old newspapers
but he got rid of the home attendant.
When he could not keep up his apartment
I found him a nursing home,
not a good one, but the best I could.

In another bout of halting breath,
Max returned to the hospital.
Before I left my job
I found him a new place—
a nursing home with concerts and crafts for patients,
nurses to help residents stay well,
real attention to detail.

Max, a Jew who escaped death
by fighting with the partisans
far from Warsaw
preferred to wangle by his wits.

I looked for him a year or two later, found him
in another nursing home a bus ride from my graduate program.
He spent lots of time on the roof
sharing his bread and thoughts with the pigeons.
And often disappeared
for walks to the little nearby stores,
dressed in his fedora,
tattered trousers and a jacket.

The Reluctant Protester, January 2018

"Somewhere I read that the greatness of America
is the right to protest for right."

Why not let others
Demonstrate, agitate, escalate?

Stretched in yoga, weekend routines we
Equivocate, abdicate, meditate.

We rely on the media and courts to
Investigate, adjudicate, mitigate.

We're overwhelmed by the acts of the 45th to
Disintegrate, contaminate, perpetrate.

The way his core of supporters
Adulate, gravitate, accommodate.

We've grown accustomed to a mind set to
Dominate, fabricate, fulminate.

On MLK day, I heard his speech evoke dogs and firehoses to
Activate, necessitate, consolidate.

At the Women's March, last Saturday,
I stood my cold ground to demonstrate.

Stand Clear of the Closing Doors

Moving to the platform
of the New York City subway,
I join the restless crowd waiting
for the next screeching train.
Doors open, I scramble
into a hard seat to read my novel,
just as four boisterous teens take
over the car's center stage
calling for our attention
through loud clapping
and clamorous rapping.

I think back to New Jersey Transit,
the passengers installed
in their suburban style row seats.
Most of the people
traveling with a companion
keep voices at a reasonable
volume. There's time
to doze or peer
through windows
glimpsing a stampede of trees,
the whoosh of commuting cars
and the beckoning skyline
of Lower Manhattan.

In front of me, as the train lurches
and shimmies, one by one,
the teens demonstrate
ornate flip turns and headstands
on the unwashed floors.
With perfect timing,

they fan out to each rider
offering polite thank yous for donations,

then, at the next station,
make their whooping exit.

Hemingway as Princeton Hair Salon Owner

My hairdresser will be running the bulls at the San Fermin Festival in Pamplona this year. He tells me this between the snips and tugs that define our seasonal ritual, when he prunes back my dense overbrush into a clean, cultivated cut. He has been doing this deed for more than a decade—me always asking him for the same service. Me, oblivious to the angles, colors, and curves of the hair captured in the pages of the trendy magazines I flipped through when I waited for Dan after he just opened his salon, struggled to pay the rent, couldn't afford to hire other hairdressers and never took vacations. Looking at the glossy photos, I would imagine letting my short, curly crop grow out and get reshaped into a tantalizing bob that looked sultry, windblown and never messy.

Dan says each morning six bulls are released into the cobblestone streets to vent their pent-up anger on the charged up throngs. And he is getting into shape by running the 826 meters that mark the distance through old Pamplona. He plans to run with a guy who did a film on the festival last year and is an expert on how to stay close to the bulls and not get trampled. Of course, the bulls are not the only ones out of control. For this reason, Dan's girlfriend has decided she will not join the thousands, mostly males steeped in wine, who push and grab as they run.

As Dan wields the noisy blow dryer with the hand of one brawny arm and lifts up my curls with the firm fingers of the other, I am thinking Ernest Hemingway and The *Sun Also Rises*. It is said that Hemingway ran the bulls two years before he published his novel, though without photos no one can be sure. Dan tells me to download an App that will broadcast videos at the same time as the event. He holds the mirror so I can see the back of my hair punked up with a surge of adrenalin.

Alis Grave Nil

Latin, nothing is heavy with wings

Light-hearted, appearance oriented,
Kis was meringue and lace,
while I preferred rye bread and fleece.
I liked tough, she sought grace.

When I battled cancer
through chemo, then surgery,
she came with me on walks,
generous with her company.

When I shared details, eager
to be honest, she said
I'm not brave like you
I'd go drawn with dread.

Three years later, her turn
to do battle, the course
much worse. We bonded as she
managed a tour de force.

She stayed light-hearted, stylish
in wigs, walked in cold or heat,
never gave in to self-pity,
her courage is what we keep.

Big Windows and a Patio to Catch the Light

My friend, the architect, is designing
a new house
for her eighty-four year old Mom.
Her Mom is ready now
to eschew space and place
down palm-lined suburban lanes
and secluded pathways,
for somewhere in town
compact and mostly on one level
within compass points
of her daily life.

Like a lively wine or robust cheese
her Mom has aged well
adding new friends and activities
to augment fallen away
people and pursuits,
resolved to remain
in the comfort of her sun
drenched surroundings,
though her daughters
and other family
are far afield.

The new home
will have a sleek kitchen
with energy efficient appliances,
yet subtly feature
a ground floor with no
barriers for a walker
or wheelchair, and grab bars
to help personal care or bathing.

There will be an upstairs bedroom
with a private entrance
from outside.

Her Mom says things like,
I need a large sink in the small
laundry to rinse out mops,
hand wash delicates.

We all want to believe
in our future.

Finley's Princeton Slaves

"Impressions of Liberty," an installation of the Princeton and Slavery
Project, November 2017

Black man in iconic hoodie,
his mission, correcting history.
Titus Kaphar, artist, featured
this month at Princeton.

Fronting the original President's House,
his sculpture is installed
beneath the sycamores,
the liberty trees
planted before the Revolution.

The silhouette of Samuel Finley,
the college's fifth president
cuts into one side of a finely constructed
sycamore box, absence
filled by glass to reveal

hidden realities,
as the changing light exposes
the etched forms of
a man, woman and child,
three of the slave family
Finley owned at his death.

Titus Kaphar, his Dad
in and out of jail,
discovered art at a community college.
His sculpture is now installed
beneath the sycamores,
summoning the dark shadows
once auctioned
under these same trees.

The Callery Pear Tree

P. calleryana trees are widely planted along streets in many urban and
suburban communities in North America

I'm ready to sprout,
not much spring is needed
to get me started.

Though you may glance
at the crocuses,
my crown of white blossoms
towers over your streets.

I hold up
my verdant umbrella
through the panting days
of summer, when my shade
draws you close.

My fall apparel
in a mottle of red and gold
never disappoints,
so everyone's eyes
fix on me, the theme
for the season. Then

dropping everything
for my long sleep,
sometimes I wear
a white cloak
or get glitzed
with winter diamonds,
but I am better off baring it.

This Is Just to Say

A Golden Shovel, after William Carlos Williams

My new passion is I
shop at Woo-Ri Mart. There, I have
discovered a new cuisine and eaten
bulgogi, Korean thin sliced beef in savory sauce. The
lure as you enter, plates of cut-up plums,
green, black and red-speckled 'dino eggs' that
float the taste buds with their juice. Were
the owners merely generous? Or did they in-
tuit the bags of plums heaped within my cart, along with the
packs of green tea mochi balls found in their icebox.

I love to travel and
how timely to have a Korean stop, which
is five minutes from my home. You
can't match Mr. Park at the fish counter bowing as if I were
a dignitary. After I stock up on crunchy seaweed, wasabi flavored,
        probably
now an addiction, I buy boxes of passion fruit juice on sale, saving
so much I can splurge for
a smoothie of banana, mint and kale, a virtuous breakfast.

If my excitement seems over the top, forgive
me or ignore me.
Such luscious Singo pears and succulent dumplings, they
rouse my hunger for new cultures. Were
Korea closer and cheaper, I'd go to take my fill of the delicious
radish kimchi fried rice and the caring people who try so
hard to make sure I bring home a ripe and sweet
honey dew melon every time, and
tell me what to buy when I can't read the labels so
I feel welcome and not out in the cold.

The Slant on Parking at the State Capitol

Ruling the underground garage, the security guard
pointed to the tight spot where she wanted me to park.
Running late, I already felt pressed,
had to assume the guard had my back.
"You have a small car so you should be able to get in."
I rounded the bend to claim the space.

Naive, I expected just enough space
sure my small car could squeeze in.
My friend, the passenger, didn't warm to such pressure,
saying she preferred to take a train, sit back,
then walk directly to the Capitol where a guard
searches for weapons, not telling her where to park.

Then I angled my car to align for the parking
between two mobile McMansions, trying to repress
dread about their intrusion into my space.
In my head, I glimpsed the pointed finger of the guard.
And I managed to inch in
too close to one side, if that driver came back

before me. Farther down the row, I spied a hatchback
next to a garden of empty spaces.
I called out to the guard.
"No way," she protested, "those spots are for the press."
Then she sneered, "If you are not planning to stay parked,
you can leave. There are visitors waiting to get in."

So I tried again despite little progress in
straightening out my approach, still not ready to back
down. And guess who appeared to coach? The guard:
"back up, back up, turn left, then right into the space."
Afraid I would shear the adjacent cars while parking,
her face screwed up as she got more and more pressed.

Abruptly, the guard hissed, "go to the section reserved for the
　　　press."
I asked "which space." She said, "any space."
A miracle after breakfast, the guard had back
tracked. With a wide smile, I drove to the eden of parking.
No problem, my car fit right in.
Persistence had yielded a gift from the guard.

At the Capitol, when you need to park and there's no space,
don't irritate the guard or talk back.
She can give places reserved for the press, then you're in.

A Daughter of Uganda in Princeton

Tritina for Jane

When I wanted to engage with health, health care and a safari in
      Uganda,
You said, I know a welcoming door there, stay with my family,
Though we were strangers, meeting at a Princeton café over tea.

Months later your sister in Kampala served me spicy African tea,
Speaking of your parents, your ten siblings, raised in a village,
      then a city in Uganda,
Before turbulent times, when you had to flee pregnant with a
      growing family.

Daffodils, balmy nights, apple cider, holiday lights, you and I
      became close to family.
You, a physician, me, a health researcher, we mulled wellness
      over tea.
You hoped to complete your treatments for cancer, then promote
      health in Uganda.

Now, your body has returned to Uganda as family and almost
      family shed tears over tea.

Grapes from the Vine

Hard Memories

In her high mood, my mother shopped.
In her low mood, she bought nearly nothing.
In her glory days, even with meds,
she amassed clothes for every occasion,
sheet music, art supplies,
and statues.

When she died, I gave away
the white marble bust of Apollo
she placed on a stand in her sunroom
surrounded by plants.
But I kept the blank-faced
child with pigtails
in a little dress.

The morning she learned she was a Grandma,
she was so overjoyed.
My father dropped her off near the bus
so she could get to the hospital,
just a half hour away, for a first look.
Five or six hours later,
she finally arrived.
She had gone from store to store
shopping for baby clothes,
telling all the saleswomen
her long-awaited news.

For almost twenty years
that little girl statue
has stood near our deck
weathering all
my Mom's unrestrained joy.

Buttoning an Era

You sent out the applications for college.
You were more than ready to leave.

Before you left, I reviewed the list of life skills
you might need. There were
ordinary skills like baking brownies,
academic skills like breaking a big project into small steps,
romantic skills like surviving rejection or breakups on your feet.

Last was sewing buttons.
I almost skipped that lesson. In your non-stop life
of homework and flute auditions, re-attaching a button
was such a trifle, a signpost from a different
age when deft stitches defined women.

Then, the buttons of your black formal jacket loosened.
Threads frayed, yet not a button lost. Had the spirit
of your grandma, a seamstress, decided
there was something you needed to know?
Two buttons detached before the audition in Chicago. The first,
I sewed, you warily watched. The second,
you "did" framed by my handiwork at the start and finish.

More buttons unhinged prior to the New Brunswick audition.
You tackled these reluctantly, me in the room for support.
Two more fell as you readied for the tryout in Montreal.
This pair you managed unaided.

The letter of acceptance finally came,
Did the sewn buttons clinch it?
Now I knew you were ready to leave.

Not the Usual Way

My parents were deep in the woods.
Dad's health was failing,
Mom, full of fears,
had treated herself
to a cocktail of bleach.
A patient on the local psych ward, she stayed
fragile though her insides had mostly healed.

My husband and I were planning a visit.
We would bring our young daughters,
finally over their sniffles and coughs,
with their giggles and chatter,
a gift to their grandpa.
And I wanted the four of us to sleep
at my parents' house.

But my husband preferred to take
my parents in small doses.
He wanted a one-day visit,
the usual length.

Like a she-wolf sensing mortal threat,
with every muscle tensed to defend
my pack,
I howled
 "We *will* stay the night."

The night of the visit,
my dad got to tickle
his granddaughters.

In the morning, he had a date
with Mom at the hospital.
It seems he left his beating heart with her.

By afternoon, I held my Mom
as I searched for a way to say
Dad was gone.

As for my husband,
I never needed to howl again.

Returns on Investment

Seven years old in Queens, NY, 1957

It was a get rich quick scheme. Our parents had agreed
to double our take from deposits of 5 and 2 cents
for large and small bottles left by workmen
at a construction site.

Those days in our town, there were no mandates
for high plywood walls to keep out intruders
or curious children. And our parents had reared us
without radar.

We searched among planks and piles of bricks
finding bottles lined against
cement foundations, half buried in the dirt,
and in tantalizing positions. Perched
on partly built floors or peering
through window frames, we swatted
to retrieve them.

Sorting our treasure
into bags, we were rich
enough to buy Milky Ways
or Snickers
and still have money
to hoard in a sock.
I saw one more bottle. Stepping
to balance on a board, I was struck
by a thick nail
punching through my sneaker
and into my foot.

After we managed to separate my sneaker
and foot
from the nailed board, I hobbled home.

First, my brother and I got our take
of quarters doubled by our parents.
Then, between a filling and a tooth extraction,
my dentist dad brought me to the doctor's office
for a tetanus shot. My biggest fear:
would my mom and dad now make me
pay the bill?

Keeping It in the Family

My father's mother Florence married
my mother's father Abe
in the living room of my parent's house
when the family gathered one wintry day.
A surprise blizzard
built barricades of snow
and no one was able to leave.
My grandmother Florence giggled that night
like a schoolgirl. She said
I spent my honeymoon sleeping
next to my children and grandchildren.

They had both outlived their calm,
yielding spouses and were lonely.
But Abe was earthy, a little unkempt,
Florence was proper, a little fancy,
and each was willful,
determined to get their way.

Abe retired from his job
driving a City water department crew.
Abe and Florence shopped, ate in restaurants and traveled.
He led the good life he never made time to do before.
When he came to visit us in fancy white shoes,
paired with new gray and white leisure pants, he laughed,
and we commented on his shaped nails
Florence covered with clear polish.

But Abe's retirement did not last long.
He found a job driving for a car service
just a few days a week.
He didn't need to tell
his family why.

Bedeviled by the Eggs

My grandfather's full, wrinkled face
with its gentle smile, was a moon
we children all looked up to.
And we were steeped in a tale
my Dad liked to tell.

During the Depression,
my grandparents had a little grocery.
they scrimped and saved,
putting in long hours,
and could not ignore shoppers
with sticky fingers.
One day my grandfather, Harry, spotted
a woman loitering in the aisle dressed
in a long, loose coat.
She tucked eggs within its folds.
Discrete and quiet,
he got out his broom,
started sweeping
and bumped her hard enough
to hear the eggs cracking.
With no words, the woman left
as egg slid down her leg
and onto the floor.

It wasn't until a decade later, studying
for a public health course,
that I wondered if there was
a different side to the story:
those good eggs scooped into the trash,
a mother left with a hungry family.

For My Cat Considers My Husband Jeffrey

For he was out the snowy evening his wife and daughters took me
  in.
For at the first glance of me he chided them for giving me warm
  milk.
For he told them to put up signs to find my prior home.
For he readied himself with gleeful expectation of my departure.
For when a blizzard buried the signs, he reconsidered my presence.
For he insisted that the others handle the duty of my feedings.
For he made sure no one forgot to give me my meals.
For he chased me into the basement before he went to sleep
  because my pre-dawn meows rattled him.
For he brought me plastic balls to push with tinkling bells inside.
For he tried to slam me with his tennis racket when I nibbled the
  juicy burgers he grilled and left on the counter for dinner.
For he rubbed the fur between my ears while he sprawled out on
  the couch to watch football.
For he and I took our naps blanketed by the afternoon sun
  streaming through the windows.
For he had me live outside when the weather warmed, a blessing
  for us both.
For no matter how far I wandered, he anticipated my hungry vigils
  by the back door each morning and late afternoon.
For he filled my bowls, set them outside the screen door and we
  both gorged on an early morning feast while he called out
  to me.
For he commiserated with me when the greedy blue jay dared to
  steal bits of my dry snacks while I preened in oblivion.
For he sprayed me with the hose if I drew too close when he was
  washing the deck.
For he laughed raucously as I dashed away feeling like a wet rat.
For he shoveled me free from the snow, plowed in front of the
  sewer, when I hid there during an unexpected snowfall.
For he always counted the days until the end of winter so we both
  could be freed from proximity.

For his patience during my last years when I could not see.

For the special way he tapped my bowl so I could hear my food coming.

For his tenderness as he brushed the tufts out of my fur when I could no longer groom myself.

For his resolve to find me after I wandered from the back of the house, growing scrawny and miserable next to a stream for days.

For the mesh and boards he used to secure the deck so I could spend my final days resting there graced by the sun and breezes.

Against the Flow

On that first weekend of Fall
when a lush September sun lulled us into believing
languid summer days would endure,
Mike, Ronnie and I were a threesome of cousins,
although you Mike
were more than a decade older than us.
We filled our bellies with heaping pastrami sandwiches at Katz's
     Deli,
then strolled for a mile or two through the gritty streets
of the Lower East Side to the Village with its trimmed trees and
     flowers
noshing on tidbits from each other's lives
stuffing our spirits with family tales.

After law school, you left the family
and went west to San Francisco where you grew
an organization seeking justice for those sentenced
to death. Through the big ears of childhood, I listened
to my parents and others fault your foresight.
Later, DNA testing stunned us,
revealing death row errors
through witnesses who claimed to see and police
who forced confessions.
When you won a lifetime achievement award
for contributions to criminal justice, colleagues
called you an inspiration and a *mensch*.

On that first weekend of Fall, you gave us
paper gifts tucked within your briefcase,
cuttings from magazines
or poems to share and talk about.

In your seventies, your tall, lanky frame, sharp eyes and fast
wit conjured youth

as did having parents who each seized a century.
We all believed you had many tomorrows.

Red Expectations

1. Unfulfilled

My husband Jeffrey bought a red Acura.
Our younger daughter Talia, the family artist,
pronounced the hue
screaming midlife crisis.
It was the car the boy wanted
and could not afford.
The man reveled in
the sporty look, the quick acceleration
and the great sound system.

But my husband worked at home,
drove modest distances.
The car's Achilles' heel was
mediocre miles to the gallon.
For a statistician, a numbers man,
each filled tank was a new test
and the car came up short.

2. Fulfilled

So Jeffrey bought a hatchback
with seats that flattened.
This new red car
became my vehicle to drive.
Almost a Valentine's Day gift
from a husband
who doesn't give flowers.
It boasted two cup holders
for coffee and a soda,

and was too bright
to get lost
in the parking lot.

With a bloom that did not wither
after a week in the vase,
it was roses
on wheels.

Different Legacies

"Doasyouwouldbedoneby" and "Bedonebyasyoudid,"
Water Babies by Charles Kingsley

When I think of my grandmother Florence
I taste the sweet rice *kugels* she carefully pan fried
for her children and grandchildren.
I see her seated at her kitchen table,
avidly reading the financial pages of the *New York Times*.
I hear her advice when she wanted me to take
a summer job with her attorney and not work
at a day camp for children with mental disabilities.
"A waste of your time," she counseled.

> When I think of my grandfather Abe
> I smell the whiskey on his breath, after he took a shot
> from the bottle my mom kept for his visits.
> I see him in his sweaty white undershirt and dark pants,
> after he mowed our lawn with a hand pushed mower,
> for he liked to be active and took pride
> in doing what needed to be done.
> I hear him talking of Mr. Brown, the man
> he routinely drove home from *Shul*
> most *Shabbat* mornings because Mr. Brown
> no longer had the strength to walk
> and no one else was willing to drive him.

After Florence grew frail
and lost her hold on reality,
her two children put her in a home
because she needed too much care.
A dozen years later, Florence had outlived
both her children. When I rarely visited her,
she was always curled up on her side. Oblivious to words,
eyes open, yet unseeing, and mute, she had become
her "waste of time."

When Abe lay in a hospital bed
in our living room, almost a skeleton,
his mind clouded by cancer, my mother
took the night shift. Everyone else pitched in
during the day to bathe, feed and chop up his meds.
When I was home, I regularly changed his diaper.
Abe had shown us how
to do what needed to be done.

Almost a Space Odyssey

In photos sent by text,
our older daughter and her husband,
aided by ropes,
hug a rocky cliff
in Yangshuo, the famed
destination in China for rock climbing,
that we never heard of,
ninety minutes by highway
and decent dirt roads
from the city of Guilin.

In the photo, my husband only sees
no helmets to cushion heads in falls,
and his collage of old TV news from China
brims with breached safety rules,
makeshift rescue devices,
and distant medical care given
only to those able to pay cash.

But I see how the cratered moonlike crust
of karst hills beckons
those reared among the can do
images of astronauts
soaring into space,
how the two young people
in the photo are thwarting gravity
and lifting themselves
higher and higher.

Watching Nomi Wrestle on YouTube

Lithe and strong, she darts below his reach
grabs the back of his thighs, hoists his body
up and over pinning him to the mat.
The ref pounds his count, declares her win.
Entangled, both wrestlers look like high school boys.
Her sex unclear when dressed in high tops, singlet,
head cap. Post-match, she frees a sweep of hair,
composed, she smiles at him and shakes his hand.

A gymnast, sprinter, tough through pain, she rose
to battle with boys in synch with those who dare
to reach beyond the myths, the leaders in red
lipstick, the combat pilots who birth their babies.
Teen still, she texts her friends and sasses her Mom.

Not My 23andMe Family

Through arrays of matched genes,
23andMe has delivered nearly 1,000 names,
it deems my family.
Usually, I let these second to fourth cousins
sharing a great or great, great
grandparent collect like dust.

When the notes of these lost cousins
show up in my inbox, I respond only to the pieces
of discovery, like Rechytsa and Babruysk,
the names of the Belarus towns outside Minsk
where my grandfather's cousins not lured
by America's promise, endured Hitler's hell.

Though my Dad revered blood relationships,
most of these gene connections
carry no memories of bloody
knees, rivalries, revelries,
proud graduations, difficult divorces.

Last weekend, I eagerly joined my second cousin Alice
and her family for a visit to Maine. (Her grandfather Sam
and my grandfather Harry were half-brothers.)

> No linkage through 23andMe, her father
> and my father were close friends in college,
> she and I lived together in graduate school.
> Forty years ago, we jogged together on weekends,
> her dog watered my rug when she (frequently)
> came home late.

Under an irrepressible sun, she waited with me when
I almost passed out climbing up Cadillac Mountain.
Striving, we all made it to the peak

to look down on the rocky ledges and the smooth seas
as we took our family photos
in front of all that could be found in the distance.

Beyond Shocking

Like artillery shattering
the clear view from my window,
the call from the gym
alarmed every cell in my body.
They said my husband Jeff
had fallen from an exercise bike
and his heart was not yet beating.

Dread dragging behind me,
I entered the emergency service
of the local hospital,
where the ambulance had taken him.
I found him on a gurney—
sitting up, thick white curls
framing his tanned, robust face.

Yet, looking confused,
Jeff asked me,
"Where am I? And what happened?"
I shared as much as I knew.
He received CPR
and five defibrillator shocks
from the gym staff before EMS arrived.
Then, when EMS gave him a sixth shock, the steady
thumping of his heart returned.
Again, my husband asked, "Where am I?
And what happened?" Again, I told him.
Once again after a few minutes, my husband asked,
"Where am I? And what happened?"
Once again, I told him.
Were Jeff and I
destined for fifty first dates?
The doctor did not know.

Airlifted to a Mecca of cardiac care,
during days and nights spent
amidst a cacophony of lights and beeps,
doctors and nurses monitored
and treated his heart,
while I stayed close
gathering the return of his memories
like a hummingbird
seeking nectar.

Dancing Out of Her Skin

Talia, June 2020

When Talia's hips snake, she leaves behind caution.
When her shoulders shimmy, she celebrates.
When she vines her steps, she turns vibrant.
When her head is flipping, her curls flying,
she overflows.

She is living *La Vida Loca* with Ricky Martin.
She *Breaks Free* to Ariana Grande.
She is sailing with the Greek, Kalidis.
She is *feeling good* to Lizzo

I'm also feeling good to Lizzo,
taking my daughter's Zumba class
from the distance of online,
she in our basement, me in the room above.

When Talia's hips snake, she grinds away resistance.
When her shoulders shimmy, she celebrates.
When she vines her steps, she turns vibrant.
When her head is flipping, her curls flying,
she's unstoppable.

Postcards from Afar

The Wonder of Eating a Naleśnik Bakaliowy in
Old Warsaw

After a cold, damp walk in Warsaw,
I entered my favorite restaurant
through a creaky, wooden door opening into
warm air, nourishing smells,
and lively conversation that needed no translation.

I devoured bowls
of steamy pierogi,
hearts filled with mushrooms and cabbage
heaped into handmade crockery.

One day I ordered a Naleśnik Bakaliowy
words I could barely say.
It arrived as the biggest surprise,
a blintze from my childhood,
my grandmother's delicacy,
a crepe encasing cottage cheese.

In front of me, this majestic blintze
covered the plate, showed itself off
studded with rum-infused raisins,
crowned with powdery sugar, laced
with chocolate. This blintze
that survived Nazi atrocities,
prevailed after fifty years of Communism,
won entrance into the European Union.

My grandmother Florence
came to America as a child
from a shtetl in Poland
and never went back.
My grandmother made that blintz
so I could.

Postcards from Auschwitz

When I visited Auschwitz
it was shrouded by snow.
The pure white that covers
my neighborhood with serenity,
here, hid ash heaved up
from the crater below.

        When I was old enough to read
        thick chapter books
        I was obsessed by Meyer Leven's *Eva*,
        a Jewish girl transformed into Christian
            Katya,
        with a false passport, her family left behind.
        Could I have dared such sacrifice?

When I visited Auschwitz
I was blasted by wind
whirling through naked branches
of birch trees masking
the ghost moans of survivors
worked to the bone.

        When I was in my twenties
        steeped in the Holocaust,
        though my parents rarely discussed it,
        I gauged Christian friends
        by whether they could be trusted
        to hide me from the unthinkable.

When I visited Auschwitz,
I was trampled by worn shoes
piled within a glass display,

the distances walked
in streets, schools, shops and kitchens,
until all paths abruptly halted.

                        When I was a parent telling my daughters
                        the origins of their Polish grandparents,
                        I found familiar last names
                        on a list of Nazi victims from Lubaczów,
                        the place of my grandparents had they not
                        come to America a generation before Hitler

when the world abandoned
its humanity,
like discarded shoes.

The Museum of Broken Relationships

The original stands in Zagreb,
a satellite in LA.
A sculptor and a film producer
recast the end of their four-year relationship
into an ongoing partnership.
A safe space to celebrate
those many loves that dared to grow,
then withered, became lost,
yet were not forgotten.

Donated objects,
each accompanied by a brief tale.
The ax from Germany:
she used to splinter
the furniture left by a former lover
into the smallest bits
after she decamped for another woman.
> The espresso machine from France:
> "He loved the coffee I made for him"
> "He loved me"
> "One day he no longer loved the coffee"
> "One day he no longer loved me."
The stiletto shoe, from Holland:
childhood passion
that flowered before its season
and ended when the boyfriend at sixteen
moved away with his parents.
Twenty years later, a dominatrix,
she made the client lick her stilettos
before whipping him.
Then, she recognized him.

The collection has been on world tours
and garnered a European prize
for the most daring museum.

From my first marriage,
I would donate
my engagement gift,
a divine necklace,
its beads, mostly black.

Flight LH403, Seats 3A & B

She knows not to speak.
A quick greeting is more usual.
Work warriors
have too much to do
to engage in banter
   with strangers.

They prepare for take-off.
He sheds shoes, puts on padded socks.
She unbuckles sandals.
Drinks are served,
the bounty of business
   with strangers.

The ship soars above clouds,
Footrests go up, seat backs recline.
He plays electronic games.
She dives into the story in her Kindle
They dine in parallel. She smiles
when their meal choices match.
He steadies her glass
   when she stands.

The cabin darkens.
They unwrap blankets,
each curl into positions seeking rest.
There will be hours of sleeping
or trying to sleep
   side by side with strangers.

Not yet morning,
the hour of arrival nears.
She opens drowsy eyes.
He eats breakfast.

She organizes.
They do not speak.
Yet she senses familiarity in awakening
  with the same stranger.

A Ghazal for Venezuela

President Maduro Denies Humanitarian Crisis

"Red Cross volunteers distributed the first shipment of
badly needed emergency supplies in Venezuela on Tuesday
after months of feuding." *Time,* April 17, 2019

A father hugs his child good night, her dwindling insulin doses, his
    nightmare.
For love of his country, Maduro turns down aid, insists "We aren't
    beggars."

A mother sells her thick, braided hair to buy rice, beans and
    chicken for her children.
With chants of *venceremos,* Maduro raises his fist: "We aren't
    beggars."

A mother grieves for her child stabbed when muggers grabbed his
    cell phone.
With hatred toward his enemies, Maduro resists, "We aren't
    beggars."

A pregnant teen reveals there were no contraceptives or money to
    buy them.
In his embrace of the dead Chavez, Maduro can't desist. "We
    aren't beggars."

Now a father lines up by a Red Cross van for water purification
    tablets.
As a maid pours his fine wine, Maduro shifts yet persists, "We
    aren't beggars."

Never Underestimate a Woman Guiding Safaris in Uganda

Lilian's bounce as she walks disarms those
who think a woman's place is close to home.
She drives the long, furrowed dirt roads with fierce
resolve, slowing for speed bumps, smiling for police
who wave her Land Cruiser through. She knows where to stop
for roasted corn unmatched in taste that's safe
to eat; she spots baboons nursing their young
close enough for a feature photo and sights
trees adorned with dozens of weavers' nests.
When her Rover rolls into a ditch, she hoes the mud
and pads the hole with branches, pacing
like a lion stalking its prey until the car is freed.

Never married, she adopted children,
siblings and singles, six in need of school,
food and shelter, her mom tends them
while she guides tourists to ensure their safety.
Lilian described a past rest day journey to find lodging
for her children and mom after a fire consumed their home,
then her faithful return to her foreign guests to show
them elephant mothers linking tails with their young
and a concert of hippos grunting and grazing at dusk.

A Day with Mifumi* Women

Babies on backs, baskets on high heads weighted with grain,
walking among the thatched huts, women stay balanced,
digging their crops, cooking in big pots, no stopping in rain.
Babies on backs, baskets on high heads weighted with grain,
when men leave, take new wives, women shoulder the strain—
village women carry on with little praise for their talents.
Babies on backs, baskets on high heads weighted with grain
walking among the thatched huts, women stay—balanced.

*a village in Eastern Uganda

Mountains Beyond Mountains in Northern Rwanda

Mountains Beyond Mountains is the biography of Dr. Paul Farmer, founder of Partners in Health. *Inshuti Mu Buzima* translates as Partners in Health in Kinyarwanda

What do you expect after an hour's drive through forests and farms
  on a dirt road?
What do you expect steering past men pushing bikes with boxes
  roped to overload?
What do you expect passing women with tall baskets on heads who
  plod bare toed?
Inshuti Mu Buzima

Do you expect a new hospital with flowers and stone walkways
  perched on a hill?
Do you expect labs able to guide treatments for diseases that would
  otherwise kill?
Do you expect staff continuously in training so care never stands
  still?
Inshuti Mu Buzima

Do you expect lodging for outpatient visits so travelers need not
  sleep in the cold?
Do you expect a place for patients' families to cook and eat while
  lives are on hold?
Do you expect counseling and support so patients in dire times can
  be consoled?
Inshuti Mu Buzima

Expect their studies to show what to change and what to grow.
Expect staff to do more for patients each year though progress can
  be slow.
Even if you expect daily rain clouds, here hope revives with each
  tomorrow.
Inshuti Mu Buzima

In the Negev with My Brother Barry
Who Lives in Israel

After the flash flood,
the River Zin reappears.

New water fills up
its parched river banks.

Amidst leafy greens,
red and yellow petals stir
like a rainbow.

Pearly white moon shells
dot the desert sand
kicking up long beached
memories.

Scat follows traces
of common thirst.

On a nearby hill,
Barry sites
our tent

so we can gaze
at the rare
rippling waters.

In the cold, dark night,
we are guests feted
by a thousand stars.

In the morning,
Barry and I balance
on sun warmed boulders
to cross the Zin

as it steadily
disappears.

San Salvador, 3,365 Miles

Our daughter's
boyfriend's father Julio
was coming to visit.

I met Julio and his wife Josefina
when I went myself
to San Salvador
to make sure
my daughter's eyes
still gleamed and her steps
had bounce
in this distant place
with a troubled past and present.

Now Julio was coming
to our house
to meet my husband Jeff,
build relationships
to support and shield
both our children.

Julio spoke little English
and Jeff spoke little Spanish
yet they connected.
Julio told stories of the Civil War
and fleeing from his house
to protect his little son.
We walked the quiet streets of our community,
he noted houses here had no high walls
to heighten safety from roving gangs.

We showed him the house
of our famous resident, John Nash,
Nobel prize-winning physicist.
Julio let us know,
Nash's wife Alicia had come,
from El Salvador,
Julio's distant homeland
that now seemed suddenly close.

Unforgettable Shopping at Cepelia, Polish Arts & Crafts

ulica Marszałkowska 99/101, Warsaw, 2007

I wanted to buy Polish pottery,
durable and practical,
in handpainted patterns
that makes everything you bake or serve
seem more spectacular.

I mulled over the selection:
squares, rectangles, ovals,
unconventional curves,
with paintings of flowers,
butterflies, hearts, and dots
in palettes of green, orange,
yellow or classic blue.

Yet the surly service
harkened back to times
when workers lorded over undeserving
patrons forced to queue for hours.
When I arrived at opening time,
the ladies were sure to make me wait
in the cold drizzle outside.
The shop had merchandise arranged behind a barrier
so the three clerks could show off
their ability to ignore any customer.
And when they finally came, they paraded
scornful looks
and shrugs of disdain.
During every trip,
they were the same.

I marveled at all the ways
they found to be rude.
Then, I would leave
to re-enter the newly Westernized Warsaw,
soothed by every fake smile,
zealous greeting and self-serving
"may I help you."

The End of My Hungarian Rhapsody

With the finish of my work in Budapest
and a train to catch
for the next day's project in Brno,
I had time for one more meal
in St. Istvan's Square
to soak up the grand Hungary of kings
and the hopeful Hungary
of reformers.
(My colleagues did not yet think
they would be rendering funeral odes
for their democracy then.)

In the glow of the midday sunlight,
I strode in the direction
of the terraced café
and recalled busy workdays
followed by stirring concerts and exhibits.
Dressed for the fall morning chill,
I wore corduroy pants, a long sweater
and bold black boots.

But crossing the street in front of my hotel
my heel caught in a crevice.
Pitching me forward, face hitting
the stone curb,
my hand twisted to the side.
A woman passerby with steady eyes
and gray hair, who spoke no English,
knelt to help me.

We took slow steps back to my hotel.
My head and hand aching,
threatened by uncertainty,
the day's melody had turned
from toe tapping *friska* to fiasco.

Khatchapuri

The iconic stuffed bread of Georgia Republic

In a stone lodge in Sveneti
at the foot of Mount Ushba,
whose craning peak
dusted by snow
rose above the clouds,

on a cold, damp day
when the electricity had failed,
we hovered near the wood-burning stove
where Varda had come to teach us
how to make khatchapuri.

For months before,
my brother in Israel and I
had planned our family trip,
our own khatchapuri
of my city odysseys through art, history,
wine and cuisine, and his treks with rocks,
trees and streams in the mountains.

We stretched the balls of dough
with pulls and tugs,
shaped it into a cup just big enough to enclose
a cache of tangy cheese
then pounded it down to a flat loaf
for memories to rise in the baking.

Secret Smiles in a Cold War

At fifty something, I learned
the art of traveling alone for a weekend in Brussels.
Mixing time alone and time with others,
I signed up for a tour bus to Bruges.

Across the aisle, a bald and bold looking man,
about my age, casually stylish,
was scanning papers from a leather file,
reading a Russian-titled paperback,

and talking periodically into his Blackberry
in Russian, of course.
To be clear, he never smiled
or turned his eyes towards me.

On arrival, the guide with his rainbow-colored umbrella
conjured up Mary Poppins
and delivered pithy tales magically in English,
French, German, Italian, and Spanish
.

always in the same order. The pattern
we followed - the Russian and I drew close
to listen to the English, surprisingly we both also
neared the guide to listen in Spanish.

Told when and where to meet the bus,
granted hours of free time,
I looked for the Russian,
though he had already vanished.

I took a boat down channels
where people hung their wet underwear
on clothes lines between two-hundred-year-old houses,
to soak up scents of fragrant air and flowers.

I rented a bike to explore the four
remaining windmills though I found only two.
Seeking a late lunch, I retreated
to an outdoor café by the path to the buses.

Approaching my table, the Russian
reappeared, smiling, offering me a beer.
The conversation veered from Bruges
to our children, he too wore a wedding band.
How did he know Spanish?
years of working in Cuba,
accompanying Cuban troops to Angola.
Our cold war thawed by cold beers.

When I looked at my watch,
it was minutes before bus time.
We flew together, searching for the hidden
location of the parked bus.

On the bus, the friendly Russian
did not sit near me, smile,
acknowledge me or say "bye."
From films, I knew the script—

cagey surveillance of Russian spies,
a too dangerous world
for easy smiles and loose talk
with an American frenemy.

In my twist of the script,
what if we had missed the bus?

Israel Beyond the Conflict Headlines

On the beach between Jaffa and Tel Aviv
waves roll toward the shore,
as families, chattering in Hebrew, Arabic,
and English, gather on the sand
or plunge themselves into the salty surf,
as we do, while lifeguards scanning the sea
bellow caution to wayward swimmers
in fluent Hebrew, Arabic and English.

We're told   Israelis, refugees
and foreign workers from Darfur,
Eritrea, Nigeria and China,
farm crops without a shared language
on a rooftop in Tel Aviv.

They speak through cucumbers, eggplants,
basil and bok choy, seeking hydroponic ways
to feed themselves and a city.

In Jerusalem, Ai Weiwei has brought
his protest art "Maybe, Maybe Not"
to the Israel Museum at the epicenter
of the Israeli Palestinian conflict
brushing aside the campaign for cultural boycott.
In one gallery, we see his 100,000 "Sunflower Seeds"
piled high like an immense thick carpet
each unique porcelain seed
handcrafted and painted,
in a propagation of classical art
over mass production.
In another gallery, we view his endless loop
of desperation from Gaza,

images of a caged tiger trying to escape
from the "World's Worst Zoo."

Later, at the beach between Jaffa and Tel Aviv,
we unwind in the routine—
lifeguards scan the sea
as families chattering in Hebrew, Arabic,
and English gather on the sand
or plunge themselves into the salty surf.

Recipes for Moving

You Do Not Have to Be a Fire to Keep One Burning

James Richardson, *Vectors: Aphorisms & Ten-second Essays, #95*

After my cousin, her mother, died,
she was a storm-tossed child,
churning in a sea of tears.
We met for lunches, walks in the city.
I brought tissues.

She became a slapdash student, with lofty goals,
enrolled at a bucolic campus college.
Her non-working dad signed loans
he could not afford.
I praised learning, implored caution.

With the threat of surging debt,
she switched to a two-year college,
became the fetching sales assistant
at a bridal salon.
I witnessed her trail lace, satin, chiffon.

Resets in retail:
she sold racy undergarments
for the non-genteel,
marketed boots, then bracelets,
handled slacker co-workers,
backstabbing bosses.
I shared ways to overcome losses.

Now she's gained entry to a four-year college.
The flame of her mother,
she's athletic, bold and witty,
We still meet for lunches, walks in the city.

The Start of Chemo after Breast Cancer Lumpectomy

The doctor put no restrictions on my activity.
In winter's cold and snow,
I
walked each day.
Yet, after my stomach settled
I
craved the stretch of watery strokes
like a tethered bird waiting to thrust her wings.

My husband
thought I was overdoing it
like a wounded bird unused to flight.
He
wanted the best for me but
He
called me crazy
and said he would not drive me
to the emergency room.

I swam
in a pool of fears.
Would my skin dry up?
Would my eyes get inflamed?
Would I catch a cold?
Would I drown?
Would I fall asleep driving the five minutes from gym to home?

He
was silent.
I
let him cool off, then
stressed my need to swim.
To appease him,

I
sent an email to the doctor—
you can determine your limits.

The following week,
I
glided with each stretched stroke
like an uncaged bird soaring.

Almost Circumnavigating the Forties

When I was in reach of forty,
my birthday present to myself
was a pair of rollerblades.
We lived in a condo off a circular drive
lined by arching trees and changing flowers
and nothing to rival gliding along the asphalt
in a steady stride, swinging my arms
from side to side,
up little hills and down the valleys,
forgetting the grip of deadlines,
my mother's meddling,
my children's "whys" and "nos."

On cold days and warm days,
in the serenity of a setting sun
or the zest of a dewy morning,
with a step into my boots and
a methodical pull of my laces,
I could roll through crises,
with toned legs and flying hair.

The girls grew up, my mother died,
my marriage survived, the job changed,
we moved houses.
I stayed on wheels until
one irrepressible Sunday in November
when I hit a rock,
hurtled across the road,
and shattered my elbow.

Almost turning fifty, was I truly
at the end
                    of my rolling road?

Judith Scott Unbound

Inspired by Judith Scott* and her art.

You
twisted
wet towels,
knotted rags,
multi-colored yarns
around the wood, wire
rubber refuse you found
in the studio or what you stole.
All disappeared into the works you
transformed with wordless intensity.
Your art wrapped in thought that spoke
every language, reflected whole truths you
did not find from teachers or books, discarded
years you were shut in an institution.
Did your spirit hibernate? Did it form a cocoon?
Somehow you stayed warm and subtle, then bloomed
when you wound shapes you could not title or define
into creations that freed your soul.

*Deaf, mute and born with Down's syndrome, Judith Scott (1943–2005) was institutionalized for decades. Her twin sister enabled her to return to the community where her art career was launched at the Creative Growth Art Center in Oakland, CA.

iStress

That puzzle of life with too many pieces.
     You can do everything—if you put it on a list.
That you can do more—if you add one more thing to the list,
     You can even add another list to the list.
That you can multitask.
     You can cook with your hands,
     plan a project with your brain,
     meet your daughter when she arrives on the train.
That you can do more if you organize,
prioritize and, of course, exercise.
That you can do laundry while you plan an agenda.
That you can stretch the day by getting up earlier.
That you can be tired but not ever quit.
That you can cycle or jog—it's essential to be fit.
That you can stay fully connected through email and text,
a virtual barrage, be ready for the next.
That you will be packed when it's time for the plane.
That no matter what
     you can pretend to be sane.

Essential Clutter

Others may stack, pack, sort,
box and toss with glee.
It really does not work for me.
There are stories in my closet
I will tell you and be honest.

Boxes of negatives with photos of my daughters at school,
when they learned to swim and raced in the pool,
if I ever have the time to look.
A basket filled with embroidery I eagerly started.
Zippers and hooks from my mother
I inherited when she departed.
The arm brace with an adjustable hinge that helped
heal my elbow broken from skating—
this year I will surely send
to a third world country.

And on a hanger covered with dust,
the black leather jeans,
I would not wear now if they fit.
I think back to the scene
when they were so slinky.

Or the gold strappy heels
that were ideal for parties
before I twisted my ankle
and chose flats as a lower gamble.

The tight designer brown boots
 I bought with my daughter
when I met her in town.
The bargain became a trance,

they just didn't fit over pants.
And I'm still looking for the perfect black dress
in brown.

Why I Never Threw out My Ice Skates

Tension is who you think you should be.
Relaxation is who you are. A Chinese Proverb

For seventeen years my ice skates stayed forgotten
stored in a garage bin, while my daughters moved out
and moved on, skating friends disappeared
and life became too imbalanced and too precious
to risk on a blade over ice.

Then, I was introduced to yoga—
a match hardly made in heaven. I struggled
sitting cross legged, balancing like a tree,
stretched in a high lunge, even in repose
with folded knees throbbing as I tried
vainly to get my bottom to rest
on my heels. Slowly, I got stronger.
Meanwhile, I learned patience, to tolerate
discomfort, to calm the mind, to breathe,
not to judge.

Grounded in yoga,
I grabbed my skates from the bin—
ready for a test at the local rink.
If I ignored the discomfort,
the ice skates still fit over gnarly feet.
Though I wobbled and lurched,
I could walk on the rubber matting.
At the border, I quaked
as if I were about to plunge
from a cliff.

Calming my mind, now or never,
I inched onto the ice,

my hand glued to the wall.
After one rotation, I dropped
the hand.
After three rotations, I managed a half smile.
After five rotations, I was gliding,
even relaxing, while gliding longer.

Afterwards, my ice skates went back in the bin.
But now they were breathing, relaxing,
secure they would not be forgotten again.

Younger, Older

My younger self did not
leave behind family and friends
journey to a remote village
in a distant country without toilets and TVs
teach English in a school, dig a well,
take pills to avoid malaria.
How I wanted to climb this Kilimanjaro.
Yet, I was caught in the gears
of my future, the tick, tick, tock
of my inner clock.

Now, I am set to climb my Kilimanjaro
with the grit gathered from falls
into ditches, with body parts
whose warranties have expired.
My scars have inspired new paths,
tracking contemporary care in East Africa
for women with breast cancer.

Before they drop,
fall leaves should blaze.

I loves you Porgy

"Porgy and Bess," New Production, Metropolitan Opera, January 15, 2020

Perched at the top of the highest balcony,
sitting amidst the camaraderie of those who bagged a diamond
at a price they could afford,
we watch the jeweled clouds descend
into regal darkness.
And wait

for the soaring, sultry notes of *Summertime*
pulling us back to that time on Catfish Row
when *fish are jumpin'* and *the livin' is easy.*
A rebirthing by stars worthy of the Met,
familiar, never forgotten songs
float us with the levity
of the human spirit
I got plenty o' nothing,
tease us with the insincerity
of scoundrels
A woman is a sometime thing,
affront us with the cruelty
of the wicked
There's a boat dat's leavin' soon for New York,
disarm us with the tenacity
of the lover left behind
Oh Lord, I'm on my way.

And after the dream,
the transit
homeward bound.
It take a long pull to get there.

On the Long Road with Philip Roth

My nemesis in the post-Portnoy age—
all the Philip Roths,
those cunt-crazy males, egos and alter egos,
who gorged on the seduction of women and girls,
as they tried to stir every problem in a woman's orifice.
I wanted no polemics against an uncaring God,
(who had already sat out the Holocaust).
I was unmoved by Roth's portrayals
of Jewish mensches and anti-mensches, standing
tall or small in Newark's cramped tenements
or its streets.

In those days, seated around a dining table
with my Brooklyn and Queens tribe,
I listened to the praise my parents, aunts and uncles
heaped on children
who toed the Jewish-American line,
who studied and graduated from
good colleges, married Jewish mates
and raised well-mannered grandchildren.

Seduced by options, not by men,
I tangled with my search for meaning
and sexual freedom inspired
by Gloria Steinem and Erica Jong,
abetted by my own curiosity and desire.
Finally, I graduated a health researcher,
married (much to my parents' relief)
the man who is still my husband.
I never deemed sex with a near stranger
(not a Russian spy or a ski instructor)
a balm for boredom or aging.

After Roth's death,
I listened to *Nemesis,* his last book,
a tale of Bucky Cantor, phys ed teacher,
director of a playground in Newark,
summer of 44,
when polio strafed its streets,
especially the schoolyard of the Jewish section
and children died or survived with maimed limbs.

Just in time for a road trip to the coast of Maine,
I had rediscovered the voice of Philip Roth,
speaking for the long, lost community of Newark Jews.
With his audiotapes strewn
in the passenger seat of my car,
I turned Philip Roth back on   LOUD.

No Still Life

The Basket of Apples, Paul Cezanne

Within an inclined basket, apples about to fall.
A wine bottle, slightly askew, towers in the center.
A multi-hued assortment of ripe apples roll
to a pause on the wooden tabletop within the folds
of a rumpled white cloth.
A blue wall.

The blue sky.
White snow covers
the folds of mountain slopes. At off angles,
skiers slide by, a multi-hued assortment.
Lift cables tower with swaying aerial seats.
In a lunge from chair to incline, I brace not to fall.

And Sew It Goes

Be sew bold
I bought the Lamborghini of sewing machines,
digital and Italian, to race down seams
and power over applique curves.

Hope sew
For the test run—three washcloth
puppets with different animal faces for a grand
nephew and cousins with new babies.

Sew much sew
The pattern arrived with sets
of shapes to fabricate brown bears,
green frogs, puppies with floppy ears.

As it sew happens
The instructions also called for fusible
net, padding and something to stabilize
decorative stitches—I hired a tutor.

Never had it sew good
By the end of my session, I had created one honey
of a bear with a fused face, padded ears,
and the most stable satin stitch smile.

I told you sew
I knew I was not alone in my gleeful folly
when I came across this quote:

> *Why buy it for $7 when you can make it yourself*
> *for $92 with supplies?*

All Small, Forgotten Miracles of Hanukkah

After "The Traveling Onion" by Naomi Shihab Nye

These are the eight days of obsession
when the lowly potato
is elevated to high cuisine.
Recipes for latkes multiply
like stars in a sky at dusk.
I search for traditional latkes
like *Bubbe* would make
even if *Bubbe* didn't cook from a recipe.
I forage for new ingredients
like leeks, sweet potato or beets
to boost color, flavor, and nutrients.

Durable Eastern European potato,
you survived the cold of the *shtetl*
as winter approached
and immigrants' passages
to new lands, merging cultures—
the seductions of hummus, tacos and spaghetti.

I sink into the dirt from ten baking potatoes
as I wash and peel their skins,
then go all in—to hand grate their firm,
bulbous flesh without donating my own.
In the battle to achieve maximum crunch,
I press the grated potato into a strainer
and pause to allow its liquor to drain out, then add
standards from eggs to matza meal,
though I texture with Asian scallions in place of onions.

Frying is always a race with time, just enough
to seal each mound with a golden crown.
At the end, I gaze at trays heaped
with dozens of crunchy latkes and wait
for my eight guests.
There is just enough time for the smoke
from my kitchen to clear the house,
another small miracle.

I Have Never Rowed a Scull

Seated in my inflatable kayak cresting the ripples
of Carnegie Lake, in a slow paddle, I chart
the shore's greenery in its turn from first gold to crimson.
When the occasional scull flies past me,
notably those piloted by silver haired women,
my imagination flutters wildly, like a ring-billed gull.
What if I owned one of those?

Yet, *whatabouts* parade like gulls—
What about the rack to hold the scull? What about
the car with roof bars to support the rack?
What about the arm and shoulder to hoist
the scull up and down the rack? And finally—
the where to find the affordable, used scull?
But let me flow with my fantasy.

A scull is the long-winged gull that transports
me to the outer banks of my imagination.
Skimming over the lake, seated in a mechanism
that orders every muscle from foot to shoulder
to orchestrate speed, I fly the lake's distance
beyond islands and bridges, clouds ogling
my performance from their perch of blue.

American Sonnet of the Vulnerable Woman

I learned to walk alone on urban streets fast
paced yuppie in the graveyard of night
dodging shadows distended near doors and alleys,
eyes stalking lighted windows in case of need

to scream in unfeigned rape culture fright.
After each late movie hanging with friends,
I ventured alone, backpack stuffed with fear,
my beating heart stoked with hope
I could elude stalkers with wiles and speed.

Now seeking nature's habitats I'm alone in the woods
tall trees spread shade while birds serenade,
paths wind over streams, frogs twang in bass notes.
Yet in the crack of a branch, the advance of a runner,
rape culture seizes me, squeezing my beating heart.

To the Sea, Ocean Grove, NJ

No sidestepping summer crowds
In October, an ocean of opportunities

Immersive solitude of bare-footed walks
Seagulls saunter, spread their wings in entitlement
Wind brushed sand rushes into footprints
Waves ferment along rocky divides
Stragglers follow waggish retrievers
Shores are bejeweled by iridescent shells
I pocket into cozy sweats over my swimsuit

The abandon of foamy surf
Do I dare take the plunge?

Backward currents from teen years
Tides of expectation
Not pretty enough   not popular enough
not athletic   nor brave enough

Now, my time to chill
    Pile of clothes left folded on the sand

About the Author

Elane Gutterman's poems have been published in *Kelsey Review, The New Verse News, Paterson Literary Review, The Ekphrastic Review* and *U.S. 1 Summer Fiction*. In 2019, she was nominated for a Pushcart Prize. This is her first book of poetry. Elane is a health researcher with a PhD in sociomedical sciences from Columbia University and an MSW from Yeshiva University. She and her husband live in Princeton Junction, NJ, where they also raised their two daughters.

About the Collection

Ten years ago, then in the midst of running a small global health consulting company, Elane faced ominous news. She had been recently diagnosed with breast cancer and was grappling with difficult treatment choices. She took a poetry class taught by Anna M. Evans at the newly opened West Windsor Arts Center, where she was a founding board member. Writing poetry helped her wade through emotional turmoil and gradually became its own channel. She crafted memoir poems poking at the synchronies and contradictions of family and community. An inveterate traveler, international journeys taken for work, pleasure and family visits, have textured her life and poetry. Also, though not athletic as a young person, she has become a devotee of physical exercise and activities in nature with a broadening repertoire as she ages. For sustenance, she swears by kettlebells as much as proper cookware.